This book belongs to

....

For my flock, Adam, George and Anna xx
C.G.

For Mrs Wilson,
S.U.

Published in 2022 by Welbeck Editions
An Imprint of Welbeck Children's Limited,
part of Welbeck Publishing Group.
Based in London and Sydney.
www.welbeckpublishing.com

Design and layout © 2022 Welbeck Children's Limited
Text © 2022 Charlotte Guillain
Illustration © 2022 Sam Usher

ISBN 978-1-80338-040-7

Printed in Heshan, China

10 9 8 7 6 5 4 3 2 1

FSC
www.fsc.org
MIX
Paper from
responsible sources
FSC® C020056

WHAT
THE
MACAW
SAW

Charlotte Guillain

Illustrated by Sam Usher

WELBECK
EDITIONS

I glide to the branch that grows over your head,
a scarlet macaw—golden, bright blue, and red.
My home is the rainforest, dense, lush, and green,
and this is the story of what I have seen...

I hatched from an egg in a hole in a tree.
My parents took care of my brother and me.
I stayed with my family 'til I was grown,
and then I met up with a mate of my own.

Now partners for life, we flew happy and free
in our forest home, which was all we could see.
We'd travel for miles to find fruit that was sweet
and swoop down to cliffs, rich with clay we could eat.

I laid my first eggs and our chicks hatched and grew,
'til finally over the treetops they flew.
But then we saw humans appear on the ground,
and soon through the forest a road snaked and wound.

Time passed and the flock was disturbed by a roar.
We panicked and rose at the sound of a saw.
We watched in despair as our trees disappeared,
our home under threat as the forest was cleared.

But then a new terror, as smoke filled the sky,
hot flames quickly spread and came roaring up high.
Our home was devoured as the canopy blazed,
the flock split apart as the forest was razed.

Our flock was now smaller, we kept on our guard,
but keeping the younger birds safe was so hard.
Now poachers would come to take chicks from their nest,
and take them away, leaving parents distressed.

Then those of us left lived in tension and fear,
we'd take flight whenever a human came near.
'Til one day, we saw a man climbing up high—
our chicks were too young to escape to the sky.

The man disappeared. I returned with my mate,
distraught at the thought of our helpless chicks' fate.
But no! They were safe, with no cause for alarm,
Their legs had been tagged to protect them from harm.

So now they are older, with tail feathers long,
it's time once again for our chicks to be gone.
My mate and I watch, as they swoop from our tree.
As they soar with the flock...

... what will they see?

Scarlet macaws have excellent vision and hearing. Their eyes are at the sides of their heads, giving them almost 360-degree vision. The macaw's good sense of hearing helps it to hear the rest of the flock communicate and keeps it alert to danger.

The hook on the macaw's beak is useful for gripping branches and bark as it climbs a tree.

All about
Scarlet Macaws

The scarlet macaw has a powerful beak with a sharply hooked tip. It uses it to peel the tough skin off unripe fruit and to break apart nuts and seeds. The macaw also uses its tongue to grind down nuts so it can digest them more easily.

Macaws can live as long as 50 years in the wild. Each macaw finds a mate when they are three or four years old. They stay together for life and rarely leave each other's side. The female lays two to four eggs every couple of years and both the parents look after their chicks for as long as two years.

Like other macaws, scarlet macaws usually gather in flocks at night to roost in the trees.

A macaw's scaly black feet are extremely good at gripping onto branches and grabbing food. Many scarlet macaws use their left foot to hold food and pick things up. They use their other foot to support them while they do this.

The macaw's body is around 3 feet (90 cm) long. The bird's tail length may make up as much as half of this. Its long tail helps it steer as it flies in and out of the forest canopy.

Scarlet macaws are very colorful birds— as well as the red feathers that give them their name, they have yellow plumage on their backs and wings and bright blue feathers on the wing tips and tail. Some scarlet macaws have green feathers on their wings and tails, too.

Other Endangered Parrots

Hyacinth macaws are the largest type of parrot and have beautiful blue feathers. They live in Brazil and Bolivia but poaching and deforestation have left them even more endangered than scarlet macaws. Only three hyacinth macaw populations now remain.

Great green macaws live in Central and South America but numbers are falling because of poaching and loss of habitat. They need tropical almond trees for food and nesting but sadly these trees are also endangered.

White cockatoos live in Indonesia but poaching for the pet trade has dramatically reduced their population.

Threats to Scarlet Macaws

In the wild, scarlet macaws live from the south of Mexico, through central American countries such as Costa Rica, Guatemala, and Honduras, to as far south as northeast Argentina in South America. Macaws are quite common in the Amazon rainforest but farther north the bird is more endangered.

Mexico

Belize

Honduras

Nicaragua

Guatemala

Panama

El Salvador

Costa Rica

Colombia

Ecuador

The number of scarlet macaws has plummeted in Central America for a number of reasons. The forests they call home are being cut down to make way for roads and farming. Forest fires have also damaged their habitat. People often light fires on purpose to clear the land for construction or farming. Wildfires are becoming more common too, because of global warming.

Peru

Scarlet macaw chicks are often taken from their nests by poachers. People can make a lot of money selling the chicks as pets all over the world, but this leaves the flock of macaws with fewer adults to mate in the future. The poachers either climb the trees to get to the nests or cut the tree down completely, causing more devastation to the birds' home and fewer places to nest in the future.

Chile

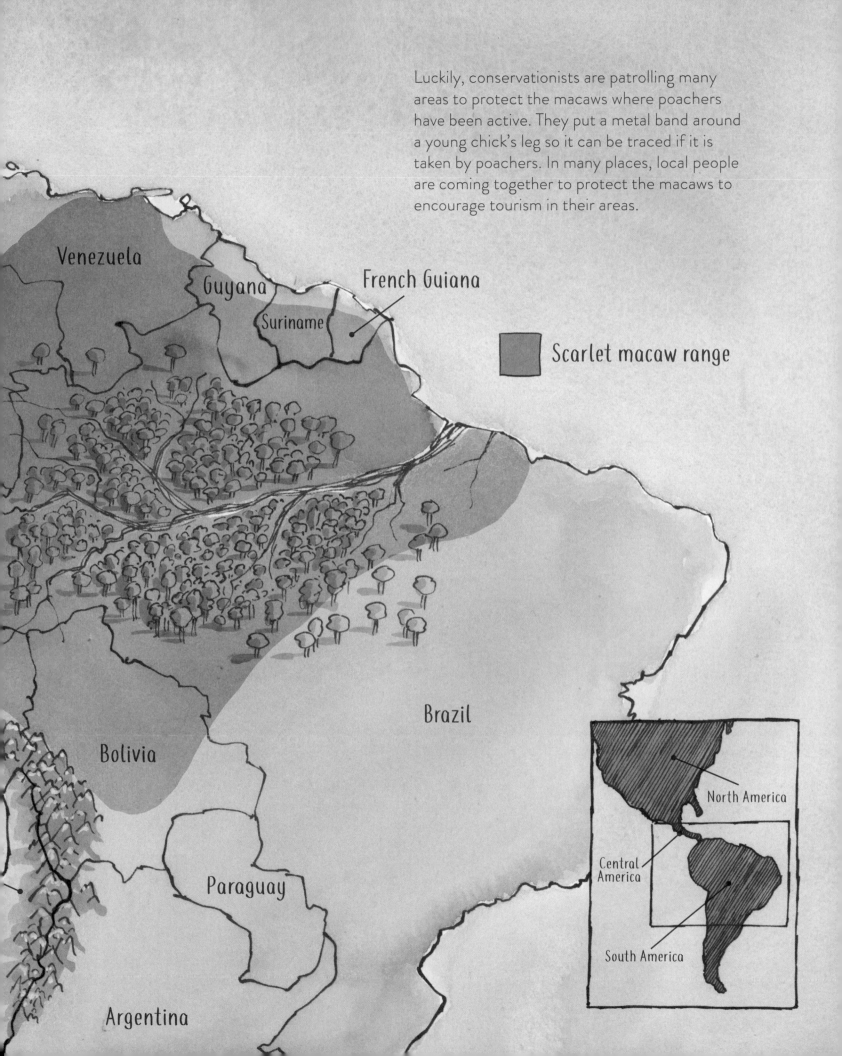

Luckily, conservationists are patrolling many areas to protect the macaws where poachers have been active. They put a metal band around a young chick's leg so it can be traced if it is taken by poachers. In many places, local people are coming together to protect the macaws to encourage tourism in their areas.

Venezuela

Guyana

Suriname

French Guiana

Scarlet macaw range

Brazil

Bolivia

Paraguay

Argentina

North America

Central America

South America

Be a Friend to the Rainforests

Rainforests all over the world need our help and protection. They are home to millions of birds, animals, and insects as well as many other living things. When trees in forests are cut down, these creatures lose their home. As well as this, more carbon dioxide is released into the atmosphere and causes global warming.

We need to slow down the rate of warming on our planet for every living creature to survive. We can help in different ways:

We can try not to buy products that contain palm oil, unless it is sustainably produced. Many forests are cut down so that palm trees can be grown for their oil. Look out for companies and organizations that support rainforests and wildlife and give them your support.

Every small thing we do to reduce our carbon emissions helps, such as walking, cycling, or taking the bus instead of going to places by car or airplane. Always remember to turn off lights and electronic devices when you're not using them.

Tell your family and friends why the rainforests need their help, too.

Be a Local
Wildlife Hero

You can also help birds and other wildlife closer to your home. Find out which birds and animals where you live are endangered and tell your friends and family about them.

If you can grow wildflowers in your garden or in a window box, you'll encourage insects. Many birds need insects as food to survive. You could build a bug hotel to give insects and other creatures a safe place to stay over the winter. It is helpful to put food and water out for birds in the colder winter months. Birds also need water in a bird bath to help keep clean. Then they can preen and spread oil across their feathers to keep them dry and warm. You could build a bird box for them to make a nest in—you never know who might choose your garden as their new home!

And last but not least, never leave litter on the ground when you are out and about—it can injure wildlife. Pick up everything you brought with you and leave things as you found them.

There might be a local wildlife organization that you can join to do more to protect living things in your environment, for example the National Audubon Society (www.audubon.org) or the World Wildlife Fund (www.worldwildlife.org).